Library of Congress Cataloging-in-Publication Data
Smith, Tim, 1945-
   Buck Wilder's animal wisdom / written by Timothy R. Smith ; illustrated by
Mark Herrick. -- 1st ed.
      p. cm.
   ISBN-13: 978-1-934133-02-6 (hardcover : alk. paper)
   ISBN-10: 1-934133-02-7 (hardcover : alk. paper)
   1. Animals--Miscellanea--Juvenile literature.  2. Conduct of
life--Miscellanea--Juvenile literature.  I. Herrick, Mark, 1950- ill.  II.
Title.
QL49.S6536 2006
177--dc22
                        2006023859

Smith,Timothy R.
Buck Wilder's Animal Wisdom
Summary:  A book about character traits of animals and how
they relate to children in real life.
ISBN 1-934133-02-7
ISBN 13    9781934133026
Fiction

10 9 8 7 6 5 4 3 2 1

Illustrations by Mark J. Herrick and EDCO Publishing, Inc.

Printed and bound in Canada by Friesens, Altona, Manitoba

A Mackinac Island Press, Inc. publication
Traverse City, Michigan
www.mackinacislandpress.com

Hi! I'm Buck Wilder and I asked all of my teacher friends for a little help in sharing the traits they like in my animal friends that best apply to the real world. So, I have gathered up my favorite animals to bring you this guide to help us understand more about nature and life, as seen through their eyes, and how it is all connected.

All things are connected.
Just ask the animals.

SET YOUR COURSE!

"HI!" I'M BUCK!

TABLE OF

| MESSAGE | PAGE # |
| --- | --- |
| BUTTERFLY — DON'T EVER, EVER GIVE UP! | 1,2 |
| PIG — CLEANLINESS | 3,4 |
| PORCUPINE — DON'T JUDGE OTHERS | 5,6 |
| ANT — TEAMWORK "ALL TOGETHER NOW!" | 7,8 |
| BEE — SHARING | 9,10 |
| BEAVER — HARD WORK | 11,12 |

# CONTENTS

| | PAGE # |
|---|---|
| **PATRIOTISM** | **13,14** |
| **LOYALTY** | **15,16** |
| **PLAY FAIR** | **17,18** |
| ·USE· **COMMON SENSE** | **19,20** |
| SHOW **EMPATHY** | **21,22** |
| **HAVE FUN** | **23,24** |
| **L♥VE** | **25,26** |

Buck Wilder

A butterfly's greatest enemy... the dreaded CAR GRILL · wim the butterfly stroke

ALMOST 3,000 MILES FOR SOME BUTTERFLIES!

ANNUAL MIGRATION ... RUN

GET EM!

Yum

Duck!

Hi!

Hi!

LET LOOSE, DUDE!

WORLDS LARGEST COLLECTION OF MONARCH BUTTERFLIES

TOURIST TRAP!

NORTH

WIND

OME ERFLIES

WE MADE IT Whew!

TO

BUTTERFL MUSEUM

SOME LIVE!

L.A. CHRYSALIS MEXICAN FOOD

BUTTERFLY BURRITO SPECIAL $5

BURRI PEREZOSO

SEÑORA BUTTERFLY'S CHÁ-CHÁ STUDIO

A GOOD WIND HELPS ME FLY!

IT'S A GREAT PLACE FOR TAKE OFFS!

MEXICAN HAT DANCE ONLY 2 PESOS

LOW

I'M DANCING

AEROPUERTO

Airport

LOW AIRCRAFT

THEY SURE DO, BUT THE END RESULT IS GREAT!

LIFE

Wheeeeeee!

WIND SURFER

DUN DA DUN DA!

GOT CHA!

Sometimes life is not fair ... but no matter what, you should never, ever give up. We are all here for a reason and sometimes our mission and travels in life are tough–there are big obstacles to get through. It takes a lot of assurance, strength, and fortitude, but the end result is always worth it.

When a butterfly emerges from its cocoon, it must first spend some time "inflating" its wings–drying them out and letting them unfold, making them vulnerable to predators. The Monarch butterfly may fly nearly 3,000 miles in its lifetime. It will travel from the far Northern Hemisphere to spend its winter in southern Texas, Mexico, or Central America. It travels through unimaginable hardships but it never, ever gives up. After a winter season of relaxation and storing up its strength it heads back north to mate, start a new family, and complete its life cycle!

BOOGIE BUG

YEE HA!

What's cook-n?

I wonder where the word butterfly came from...

"Wash your hands before you eat, sit up straight at the table, elbows off, and don't eat like a pig!" I heard those words often growing up. "Brush your teeth, clean your room, and clean up that attitude." I'm sure you've heard these words too. We often refer to the opposite of cleanliness as living like a pig. Anything in this scene look familiar? Take a good look.

Pigs, believe it or not, are not the dirtiest, sloppiest animals around.

They are very intelligent, learn quickly, and given the choice, will keep themselves extremely clean. They like to roll in the mud to cool off their bodies because they don't sweat. The mud provides protection against insect bites and possible sunburn. That's why pigs always look dirty! I wonder if the sun-screen lotion we use would work on a pig's body? Remember pigs have to get dirty for survival- you don't!

**PIG** thief?...A **HAM**-burglar! **PLAY** this little piggy went to the **MARKET**

# DON'T JUDGE OTHERS

There is an old saying that says "Don't judge others until you have walked a mile in their shoes." Keep an open mind about people, their differences, their looks, their opinions, and their actions. We are all different on this earth. Respect that, learn from it, and don't judge others.

The porcupine is a good example of 'not judging others.' Just because they are covered with prickly little spikes doesn't mean that they are a mean and ornery animal. Their quills are just for defense. Porcupines are a salt-loving animal, they move slow, and don't mean harm to anyone.

You will always accomplish more in a shorter period of time by utilizing teamwork instead of trying to do it all by yourself. Teamwork is working together to accomplish the common goal. Remember, in the end give the credit to the team and not just to an individual.

If you ♈♈ Leave nature alone, it will balance ♈ out.

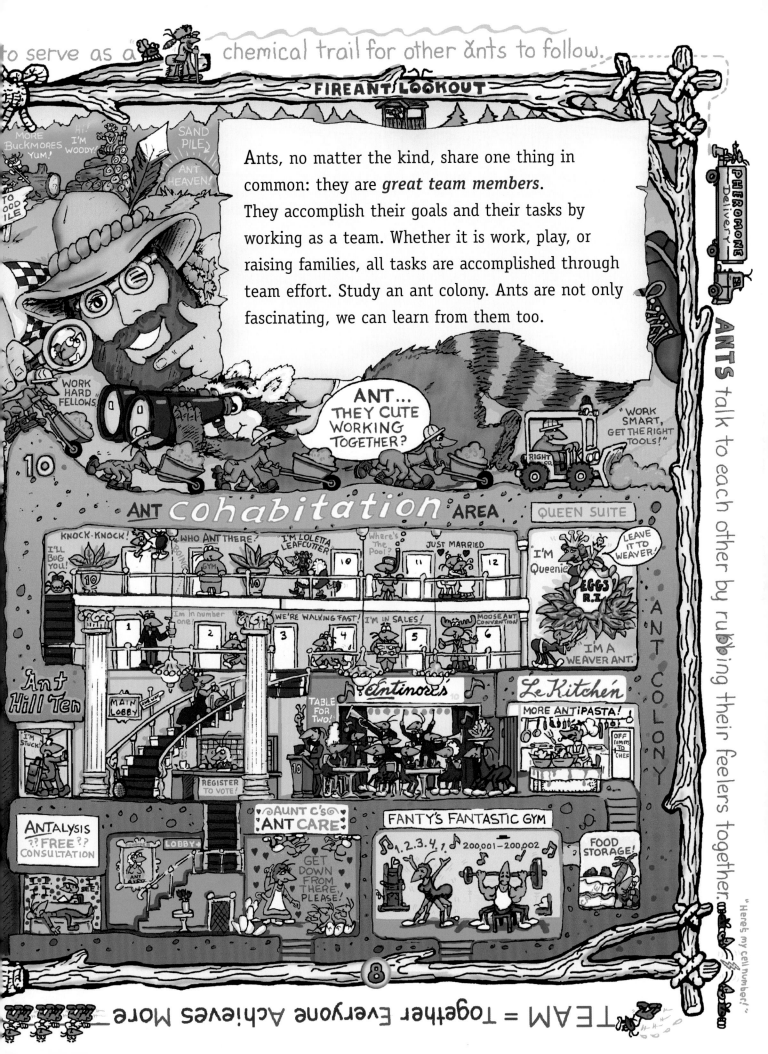

Ants, no matter the kind, share one thing in common: they are *great team members*. They accomplish their goals and their tasks by working as a team. Whether it is work, play, or raising families, all tasks are accomplished through team effort. Study an ant colony. Ants are not only fascinating, we can learn from them too.

TEAM = Together Everyone Achieves More

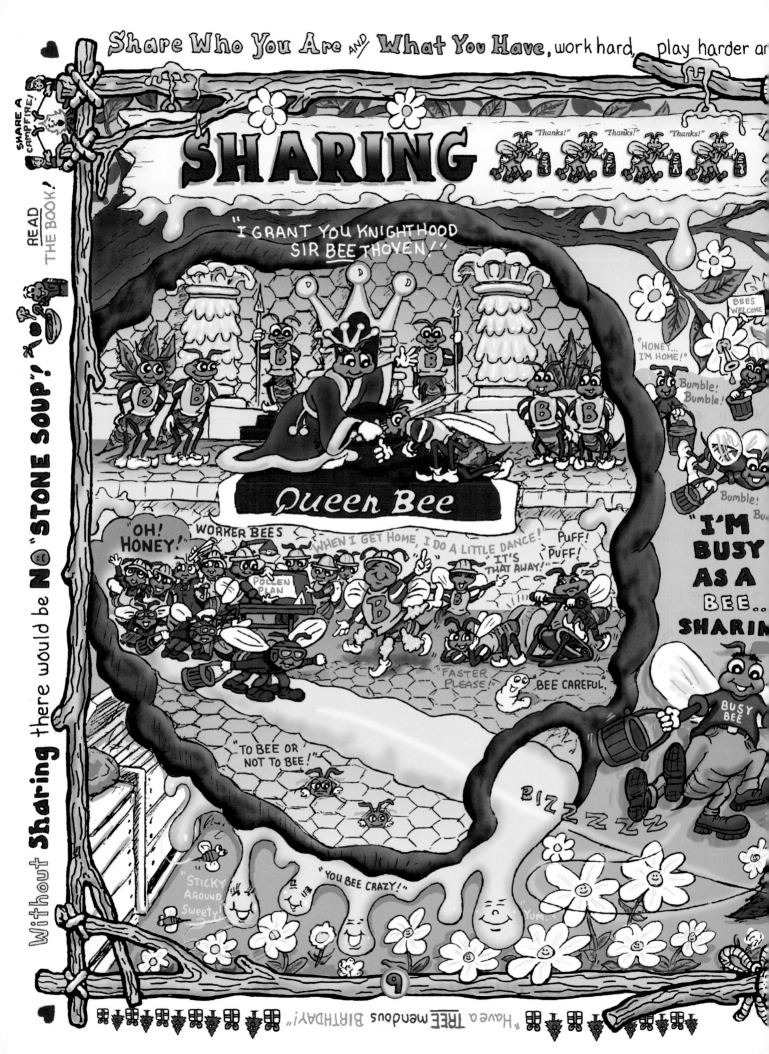

This is a "GREAT" story  Pollinating is FUN!
BEE cause...

EUUUTIFUL NATURE!"

"RASCAL, BEES ARE VERY IMPORTANT TO OUR WORLD!"

"SWEET."

BEE BONNET

OFFICAL BEE-LINE!

COWBOY BEE "YEE HA!"

HONEY I'M GOOD FOR YOU!

Sharing is using something with someone else, giving something of yours to someone else, or taking turns. Sharing is caring. The ability to give someone else something of your own—your time, your love, half of your sandwich—means you care for that person. It is very true that by helping others you help yourself. You are rewarded in many different ways and it makes your heart feel good.

The lives of bees are fascinating, especially honey bees. They are sharing, giving creatures that ask little in return for all the work they do. They work hard all day, sun up to sun down, gathering nectar from flowers to make honey in their hives to share with their bee brood. In the process they pollinate our flowers, plants, and fruit trees and they get it all done in a very short life span.

CLOWN DAISY

10

When I think of a beaver I think of an animal that works very hard, almost constantly. It is hard to imagine how they build their beaver dams with such strength and intricacies to hold back the force of water. Through hard work a beaver utilizes its natural resources to its greatest potential.

There is no substitute for hard work. Don't wait for opportunities to come knocking at your door–go out and make things happen! Working smart in combination with working hard will bring you fulfillment, satisfaction, and a sense of accomplishment. Have no fear of it … it's good for you!

# PATRIOTISM

REMEMBER FLAG DAY

The Great Wing Stadium

FURRY CUP WILDERNESS CHAMPIONSHIP

OTTER GUYS

"WE'RE FROM THE SAME SCHOOL!"

NICE ICE!

"WE PREFER SPUMONI MACHINES!"

AL →

STROMBOLI

"GO U.S.A.!"

GO BEAVERS PADDLE EM!

← GO THE OTTER WAY! →

FUR THE WINNERS

WAYNE GRIZZLY

WILDER STICK A

HOME

PENALTY

SCORE KEEPER
NO STINKY CALLS

Patriotism is loving and having loyalty to our country. We express patriotism in many ways: through our Pledge of Allegiance, facing the flag, by celebrating Independence Day on July 4th, and by flying our flag with pride, etc. Many people have sacrificed their lives through patriotism for our country.

stand up, face the **FLAG**, and put your right hand over your heart.

played ♫, **STOP** what you are doing, **DON'T** talk, take your hat

BIG BEAVERS VS. OTTER GUYS

I PLEDGE ALLEGIANCE...

Buck Wilder HOCKEY

OTHER OTTER GUYS

SOUVENIRS

BEAVERS

BUCK B.

BIG DEALS! BY WILBUR FAKE

SECTION I-C

BEAVERS ARE THE WORLD CHOMPIONS

"HEY LOUIE, WHICH WING?"

"WE BELIEVE IN A COUNTRY WITH VALUES!"

AERIE

"I'M A RED WINGS FAN!"

NALTY CANCY

VISITORS

GORDIE HAWK

"GOOD SPORTSMANSHIP IS THE AMERICAN WAY!"

"I WAS TOO WILD FOR THE JOB!"

1ST RUNNER UP

DON'T LIE!

One of the most patriotic symbols of our country, other than our flag or maybe the White House, is the Bald Eagle. It is an American symbol that represents freedom, strength, endurance, and majesty. Chosen by our Congress in 1782 as the national symbol, it barely beat out the second choice–the wild turkey–which was Ben Franklin's first choice!

# LOYALTY

is the ancestor of all dogs.

The WILD WOLF

"WE GO WAY BACK!"

WOO WOO!

B THE DOG GONE INN

BowWowery Hotel

B

"MRS. KENNEL, WE HAVE ARRIVED!"

"What a dog day afternoon."

"ARRIGHT!"

OFF LIMITS

Pointer

"HERE KITTY... KITTY!"

NW

TRASH

1st OLD IT OI TIM

"DO WE LOOK ALIKE?"

"HELLLP!"

Yo!

CLUCK! CLUCK! CLUCK!

"I'M SEEING SPOTS!"

"It is said... dogs look a lot like their owners."

LEW

"HE SAVED ME!"

Central

Loyalty is being faithful, trustworthy, and true. Whether it be to yourself or to others, when you are loyal you can be depended on for support. Friends recognize your loyalty when they can safely trust and confide in you.

A dog is man's best friend, period! No matter the size, shape, color, or breed, you can find no better animal friend than a dog. The bond between a man and his dog is one of trust and respect. Remember to always hold that trust in the highest regard and your dog will be your friend to the end! There are endless stories written about dogs–*Lassie*, *Old Yeller*, *The Incredible Journey*, etc. Make time to read some of these exciting classic stories.

Throughout our lives we have many opportunities to make the call—safe or out. The best rule to follow is to make the call as you would make it for yourself. Be fair to others as you would be fair to yourself. Always play by the rules, be fair, and your problems will be few.

A fox is a very cagey, smart, and cunning animal that may not seem that fair. He'll dress up in sheep's clothing and steal your chickens before you know it. A wolf will come knocking at the front door, but a fox will always try to sneak in the back. You may meet people in your life who act a little fox-like—remember this story and guard your chickens.

**PRODUCT DESIGN AND TESTING**

GET YOUR COMMON SENSE IN GEAR!

COMMON SENSE TOY FACTORY
"We Build Toys That Make Sense."

PONY RIDES 10¢
COMPANY TOURS FREE!

THIS LIST MAKES SENSE!

CHECK LIST

RECYCLED WOODCHIPS

REUSE STUFF YOU'LL GET RICH!

It is usually thought that a wise person is one who has a lot of common sense and makes good judgments. Common sense is simply the ability to think straight and see things in a clear manner. The old adage, "The shortest distance between two points is a straight line," best exemplifies common sense. Look at things clearly and apply what you've learned in life in a logical manner.

Most often we look at the "wise old owl" as representing wisdom and common sense. In cartoons and books it is usually portrayed as the wise old judge in horned rimmed glasses being the "explainer of all". Owls really are very smart for you'll rarely see one in the wild. They use their wisdom and knowledge to stay safe from enemies.

THIS MAKE SENSE ⇨

REMEMBER, nature is always right and flowers are the smile

THINK before you ACT! Life is all about choices!

# SHOW EMPATHY

The FIRST ANNUA...
MASQUE...

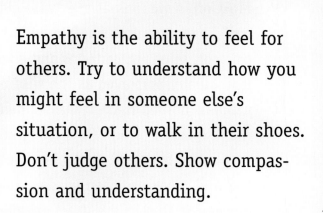

Empathy is the ability to feel for others. Try to understand how you might feel in someone else's situation, or to walk in their shoes. Don't judge others. Show compassion and understanding.

Looking at a skunk is a great test of your empathy – pee-yew! Can you feel for the skunk and the life he must lead? Who is going to invite Mr. Skunk to their house for dinner, family game, or social event? In reality a skunk is a very easy going animal with a good disposition and generally prefers to be left alone.

If you are ever lucky enough to see an otter in the wild, you'll see a cute little furry animal that works hard and plays hard. Otters tend to have the most fun with what they have. Whether they are swimming upside down, breaking shells on their stomach, or sliding down a mud hill, they seem to do it with a chuckle.

**OTTERS HAVE SO MUCH FUN!**

"YES, WE DO!"

"I WANT TO JOIN 'EM, BUCK!"

FLOP! FLOP!

MUDS UP DUDE!"

RENTAL MUD RIDES

BUMPER MUD BOARD

"H-O!"

Life would be so boring if we couldn't have fun. Having fun allows us to enjoy life, to play, and to laugh. There are times it will take you away from the routine, the dull, the difficult, and the boring. The best person to have fun with is you. It is okay to laugh at yourself or your own jokes. Fun is what you make of it. Just watch, fun is right around the corner.

RIDE THE FAMOUS MUD SLINGER II

"ONLY 1 FISH TO RIDE!"

FRESH FISH

SALE

"IF ITS BIG ENOUGH!"

SLINGER II

STOP ! Go the "OTTER WAY!" NOT this way...

It's OK to show your emotions · Tears show your emotions

# L♥VE

"AHOY MATE!"

THE WORLD NEEDS LOVE!

WE BE JAMMON!

DO THE LOVE SHAKE!

A LITTLE TURKEY WITH LOTS OF SAUCE!

SHE EATS LIKE A BIRD!

JIMMY'S BUFFET - EAT MORE, PLAY MORE!

WARNING

1 L♥VE

BOB

READ... THE OLD MAN AND THE SEA!

THOSE THAT CRU

PIRATES OF HEARTS

L♥VE BO

( S.S. WILDER CRUISES )

"I STEER!"  "WE PADDL

To have a loving spirit, to act in an affectionate loving way, to be soft, gentle and pure ... to be in love. It comes in different feelings, ways, and shapes but you can always recognize it when you see it. There are more books written, songs sung, and stories told about love than any other subject – because true love is almost indescribable. Love can be found in many places.

It has been said that "love makes the world go round" and love can surely be found throughout the world in both humans and animals. There are many kinds of love. A mother's love for her child, a child's love for his or her parents, the love for a pet, and the love for friends are only a few of the many examples. Love can also be shown in many ways. It can be shown through protection, compassion, kindness and doing things for others. Love is one of the most intense feelings we might ever have and the *greatest gift we can give*.

A good measure of a person's REAL character IS

NAG: NAG: NAG:
reaper!

ELEMENTARY

HAVE GOOD MANNERS!

BE HONEST!

I HONESTLY LIKE THIS ONE, BUCK!

PLAN AHEAD!

BE RESPECTFUL!

BE CARING!

BE PATIENT.

Listen to your ELDERS!

TRY NEW THINGS!

BE RESPONSIBLE!

I'm really glad you joined my animal friends and me on this unique outdoor adventure. I hope you had fun reading about their animal antics, natural wisdom, and cool traits. If you liked *Animal Wisdom*, you will want to share other fun outdoor adventures with Rascal Raccoon and me in my *Small Fry Fishing Guide*, *Small Twig Hiking & Camping Guide*, and *Little Skipper Boating Guide*. And be sure to watch for my new and exciting *Buck Wilder's Adventures* chapter book series coming very soon. The first three: *Who Stole the Animal Poop?*, *The Work Bees Go On Strike* and *The Ants Dig to China* are mysterious and amusing!

Thanks,
Buck Wilder

But that's not all, there are plenty more coming, so keep your eyes open for more *Buck Wilder's Adventures*.